No part of this work may be reproduced, incorporated into a computer system, or transmitted in any form or by any means (electronic, mechanical, photocopying, recording or otherwise) without the prior written permission of the copyright holders. Infringement of such rights may constitute an intellectual property crime.

ISBN: 978-91-89848-87-0

Will you help us? Let's Save Endangered Animals © Grete Garrido, 2025

THIS BOOK BELONGS TO:

THE EARTH IS A WONDERFUL PLACE, ISN'T IT?
ESPECIALLY BECAUSE YOU ARE HERE! AND ALSO BECAUSE OF ALL THE DIFFERENT CREATURES THAT LIVE HERE WITH US.

WE ANIMALS LIVE ON EARTH TO ENJOY LIFE, PLAY, AND WATCH OUR FAMILIES AND FRIENDS GROW, JUST LIKE YOU!
BUT UNFORTUNATELY, SOME HUMAN BEHAVIORS ARE CAUSING MANY OF THE AMAZING ANIMALS THAT SHARE THIS PLANET WITH US TO BE ON THE BRINK OF DISAPPEARING.
AND WE CAN'T LET THAT HAPPEN, CAN WE?

IN THE NEXT PAGES, SEVERAL ANIMALS THAT ARE IN DANGER OF EXTINCTION ARE GOING TO TELL YOU SOME OF THE THINGS THAT MAKE THEM SO SPECIAL.

AFTER GETTING TO KNOW THEM BETTER, WE'RE SURE YOU'LL LOVE THEM EVEN MORE AND YOU'LL FIGHT FOR THEM TO KEEP LIVING ON EARTH FOR MANY, MANY MORE YEARS!

WE SHARE UP TO 98% OF OUR DNA WITH HUMANS— WE'RE ONE OF THE SPECIES MOST LIKE YOU. HI, COUSIN!

SO, IT'S NO SURPRISE THAT WE CAN SHOW A SENSE OF HUMOR, FEEL SADNESS, PLAN AHEAD, AND HAVE AMAZING MEMORIES.

I'M AS STRONG AS 4 TO 8 GROWN MEN!

WE COMMUNICATE IN MANY WAYS: THROUGH GESTURES, BODY POSTURES, FACIAL EXPRESSIONS, VOCAL SOUNDS, CLAPS, AND EVEN SCENTS.

WHY DO WE BEAT OUR CHESTS? IT'S A SHOW OF STRENGTH! THE DRUM-LIKE SOUND TELLS OTHERS WE'RE STRONG AND HEALTHY, SO THEY THINK TWICE BEFORE BOTHERING US.

THERE ARE ONLY ABOUT

1.063

MOUNTAIN GORILLAS LEFT IN THE WORLD

I'VE BEEN AROUND SINCE THE TIME OF THE DINOSAURS!

I'M NOCTURNAL, SNEAKY, AND SHY.
I FIND MY WAY USING MY SENSE OF SMELL AND SHARP HEARING.

I'M AN EXCELLENT SWIMMER AND CAN EVEN FLOAT IN WATER BY TRAPPING AIR IN MY INTESTINES.

I HAVE SHARP CLAWS THAT I USE TO DIG BURROWS UNDERGROUND AND TO FIND ANT NESTS. YUM!

WHEN I'M SCARED, I CAN JUMP NEARLY THREE FEET INTO THE AIR!

I CAN SLEEP FOR MORE THAN 16 HOURS A DAY. ZZZZZZZZ...

THERE ARE ONLY ABOUT

3,500

GIANT ARMADILLOS LEFT IN THE WORLD

I'M THE LARGEST ANIMAL ON THE PLANET.
MY TAIL FINS CAN BE AS WIDE AS A SOCCER GOAL.

MY HEART IS ENORMOUS! IT CAN WEIGH CLOSE TO 2,000 POUNDS. IT BEATS ONLY ONCE EVERY 10 SECONDS AND CAN BE HEARD FROM 2 MILES AWAY. KEEP AN EAR OUT WHEN YOU'RE DIVING!

WHEN WE SURFACE, WE EXHALE AND THEN INHALE ENOUGH AIR TO FILL A TRUCK—IN JUST 1.5 SECONDS.
WE DO THIS THROUGH A BLOWHOLE ON TOP OF OUR HEADS, AND WE CAN SHOOT WATER UP TO 40 FEET HIGH.

WE HAVE AMAZING LUNGS. HUMANS CAN HOLD ABOUT 6 LITERS OF AIR, BUT WE CAN HOLD 5,000 LITERS (1,320 GALLONS).

THERE ARE ONLY ABOUT

10,000 y 25,000

BLUE WHALES LEFT IN THE WORLD

DO YOU LIKE BALLS? WE DO TOO! WE LOVE MAKING "LEMUR BALLS," WHERE WE SNUGGLE TOGETHER TO SLEEP AND KEEP WARM.

IN THE MORNING, WE SUNBATHE IN A POSITION LIKE THE "LOTUS POSE."
WE USUALLY DO THIS IN GROUPS. OOOOOOMMMMH…

SMELL IS SUPER IMPORTANT TO US! THE SCENT FROM THE FEMALES TELLS US ALL KINDS OF THINGS—LIKE IF THEY'RE FERTILE, PREGNANT, OR EVEN THE GENDER OF THEIR BABY.

MOST OF US LIVE IN MADAGASCAR. DO YOU REMEMBER US FROM THE MOVIE?

THERE ARE ONLY ABOUT

2,500

LEMURS LEFT IN THE WORLD

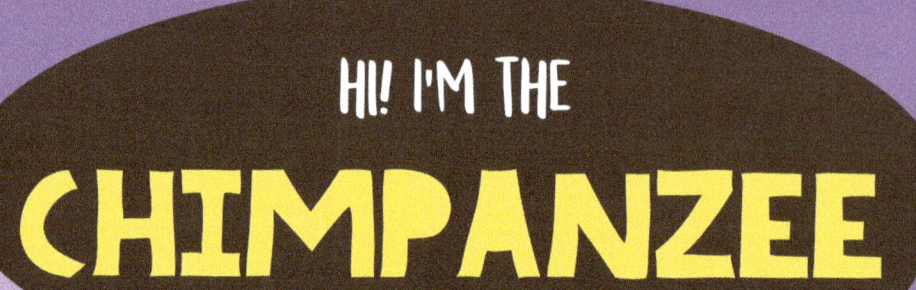

Just like you, we give kisses, hugs, and even tickle each other... and yes, we laugh when we play too!

When we get bored, we invent games.
I bet you do the same with your friends!

We're super social and live in communities of up to 150 chimpanzees.

We love sleeping comfortably.
Every night, we build "nests" to sleep in.
Sometimes, we even make a pillow out of the softest leaves.
We rarely sleep in the same nest twice!

We eat with our hands and can throw objects or even create tools.

There are only about
150.000 / 200.000
common chimpanzees left in the world

OUR TEETH CHANGE ABOUT 6 OR 7 TIMES DURING OUR LIVES—NOT JUST ONCE LIKE HUMANS. THE TOOTH FAIRY WANTS NOTHING TO DO WITH US!

WE ARE EXTREMELY INTELLIGENT ANIMALS, WITH A BRAIN THAT WEIGHS 11 POUNDS. WE CAN UNDERSTAND MORE THINGS THAN ANY OTHER ANIMAL, EXCEPT WHALES.

WE SPEND MORE THAN 16 HOURS A DAY EATING. EVERY DAY, WE MUNCH ON ABOUT 440 POUNDS OF FOOD!

OUR TRUNK IS AMAZING. IT HAS OVER 3,000 MUSCLES, WITH THE PRECISION TO PICK UP A COIN AND THE STRENGTH TO LIFT A TREE TRUNK. IT'S BOTH MY NOSE AND UPPER LIP, AND I USE IT FOR EATING, DRINKING, SMELLING, BREATHING, AND EVEN MAKING SOUNDS.

THERE ARE ONLY ABOUT
415,000
AFRICAN ELEPHANTS LEFT IN THE WORLD

OKAY, I ADMIT IT, I'M A BIG SLEEPYHEAD!
I SLEEP ABOUT 20 HOURS A DAY, BUT I HAVE A GOOD EXCUSE—MY DIGESTION IS SUPER SLOW! THAT'S WHY I'M SO LAZY.

I ONLY EAT EUCALYPTUS LEAVES. I MUNCH ON ABOUT 2 POUNDS A DAY, AND JUST IN CASE I GET HUNGRY LATER, I STORE A FEW LEAVES IN MY CHEEKS.

FOR THE FIRST 6 MONTHS OF OUR LIVES, WE STAY IN OUR MOM'S POUCH. THEN, FOR THE NEXT 6 MONTHS, WE EITHER RIDE ON HER BACK OR GO BACK INTO HER POUCH.

WE DON'T DRINK WATER, UNLESS WE'RE SICK. WE GET ALL THE WATER WE NEED FROM THE EUCALYPTUS LEAVES.

THERE ARE ONLY ABOUT

80.000 / 170.000

KOALAS LEFT IN THE WORLD

I'm the largest cat in the world and can weigh up to 815 pounds!

Not to brag, but I'm also the mammal that can jump the highest— I can leap as high as 16 feet.

Our stripes, just like your fingerprints, are unique to each tiger. No two tigers have the same stripes.

We can run as fast as 56 miles per hour.

Our roar contains a type of infrasound that humans can't hear, but it has terrifying and paralyzing effects! Grrrrrrr!

There are only about **5,574** tigers in the world

Hi! I'm the RHINOCEROS

There are 5 species of rhinos: white, black, Javan, Indian, and Sumatran.

We can survive up to 5 days without drinking water.

Our front horn keeps growing throughout our lives. The largest horn ever recorded was 5.2 feet long—probably longer than you are!

Our eyesight isn't great, but we have a fantastic sense of smell and hearing to make up for it.

If a baby rhino is threatened by a predator, the adults form a circle to protect it.

There are only about **27,000** rhinos left in the world

WE'RE GREAT SWIMMERS AND CAN SWIM ANYWHERE FROM 19 TO 62 MILES WITHOUT STOPPING.

WE'VE ADAPTED TO LIVE IN -22°F IN THE NORTH POLE.
OUR SECRET TO SURVIVING THE COLD? A THICK LAYER OF FAT ABOUT 4 INCHES DEEP AND FUR THAT REPELS WATER.

WE EAT ABOUT 66 POUNDS OF FOOD EVERY DAY—THAT'S A LOT!

WANT TO BE AMAZED? WE'RE NOT ACTUALLY WHITE!
OUR FUR IS TRANSLUCENT. BETWEEN THE HAIRS ARE LITTLE AIR POCKETS THAT REFLECT LIGHT, WHICH MAKES US LOOK WHITE. DEPENDING ON THE SUNLIGHT OR THE TIME OF YEAR, WE CAN EVEN LOOK YELLOWISH OR BROWNISH!

THERE ARE ONLY ABOUT

30.000

POLAR BEARS LEFT IN THE WORLD

HI! I'M THE
GIRAFFE

WE SPEND MOST OF OUR LIVES STANDING UP—EVEN WHEN WE SLEEP!

WE'RE SUPER TALL, MEASURING BETWEEN 13 TO 20 FEET. OUR TONGUES ARE SO LONG THEY CAN STRETCH UP TO 20 INCHES.

BECAUSE WE'RE SO TALL, OUR BABIES GET A ROUGH WELCOME TO THE WORLD—THEY FALL MORE THAN 5 FEET WHEN THEY'RE BORN.

LUCKILY, GIRAFFE CALVES CAN STAND UP AND EVEN RUN JUST AN HOUR AFTER BEING BORN.

A KICK FROM ONE OF OUR LONG LEGS CAN BE VERY POWERFUL. IT CAN SERIOUSLY INJURE OR EVEN KILL A LION!

THERE ARE ONLY ABOUT
117,000
GIRAFFES LEFT IN THE WORLD

WE'RE MASTERS OF CAMOUFLAGE AND PERFECTLY EQUIPPED TO LIVE IN THE MOUNTAINS.

MY LONG, THICK TAIL SERVES TWO PURPOSES.
IT HELPS ME KEEP MY BALANCE ON STEEP, ROCKY SLOPES, AND I CAN ALSO WRAP IT AROUND MY BODY TO KEEP WARM DURING THE COLD WINTER.

WE'RE ONE OF THE FEW BIG CATS THAT DON'T ROAR.

WE LIVE HIGH IN THE HIMALAYAS AND THE MOUNTAINS OF CENTRAL ASIA, AT ALTITUDES BETWEEN 6,600 TO 19,700 FEET.

THERE ARE ONLY ABOUT
6.500
SNOW LEOPARDS LEFT IN THE WORLD

WE DIVE UP TO 300 FEET UNDERWATER TO FIND FOOD.
IF WE CAN'T OPEN THE SHELLS OF OUR PREY WITH OUR CLAWS, WE USE ROCKS TO CRACK THEM OPEN.

OUR WHISKERS ARE VERY SENSITIVE, AND THEY'RE ONE OF THE MAIN SENSES WE RELY ON TO FIND FOOD.

WE'RE VERY AFFECTIONATE AND SHOW EACH OTHER LOVE ALL THE TIME. WHEN WE SLEEP ON LAND, WE LIKE TO HUG ANOTHER OTTER TIGHTLY TO KEEP EACH OTHER SAFE. AND WHEN WE SLEEP IN THE WATER, WE HOLD HANDS SO WE DON'T DRIFT APART.

AS WE GET OLDER, OUR FUR TURNS WHITE.
WHEN THIS HAPPENS, THE OTHER MEMBERS OF OUR FAMILY TREAT US WITH MORE RESPECT AND GIVE US THE BEST FOOD.

THERE ARE ONLY ABOUT

300.000

OTTERS LEFT IN THE WORLD

Brown bears aren't always brown!
We can be red, brown, cream, bicolored, or almost black.

We are the largest land mammal in Europe!

I live in the forests and mountains of North America, Europe, and Asia.

Even though we have a reputation as fierce carnivores, we actually get up to 90% of our calories from plants. Yum!

Baby brown bears are born blind and weigh only 340 to 680 grams (about the weight of a loaf of bread!). Our cubs grow quickly and reach 55 pounds by six months old.

There are only about **200.000** brown bears left in the world

I'M ONE OF THE OLDEST ANIMALS ON EARTH—I'VE BEEN LIVING ON THIS PLANET FOR NEARLY 35 MILLION YEARS!

OUR DISTINCTIVE BLACK AND WHITE COLORING HELPS US CAMOUFLAGE IN THE UNDERBRUSH OF SHADOWY PLACES.

I HAVE A SHARP SENSE OF HEARING AND SMELL, WHICH IS SUPER HELPFUL FOR FINDING FOOD, DETECTING DANGER, AND LOCATING OTHER TAPIRS. IN FACT, MY HEARING AND SMELL MAKE UP FOR MY POOR VISION.

I'M DISCREET, SOLITARY, AND HARMLESS, WITH SIMPLE HABITS.

I HAVE AN ELONGATED SNOUT, KIND OF LIKE A TRUNK, WHICH HELPS ME FEED ON ROOTS AND LEAVES.

THERE ARE ONLY ABOUT

5.000

TAPIRS IN THE WORLD

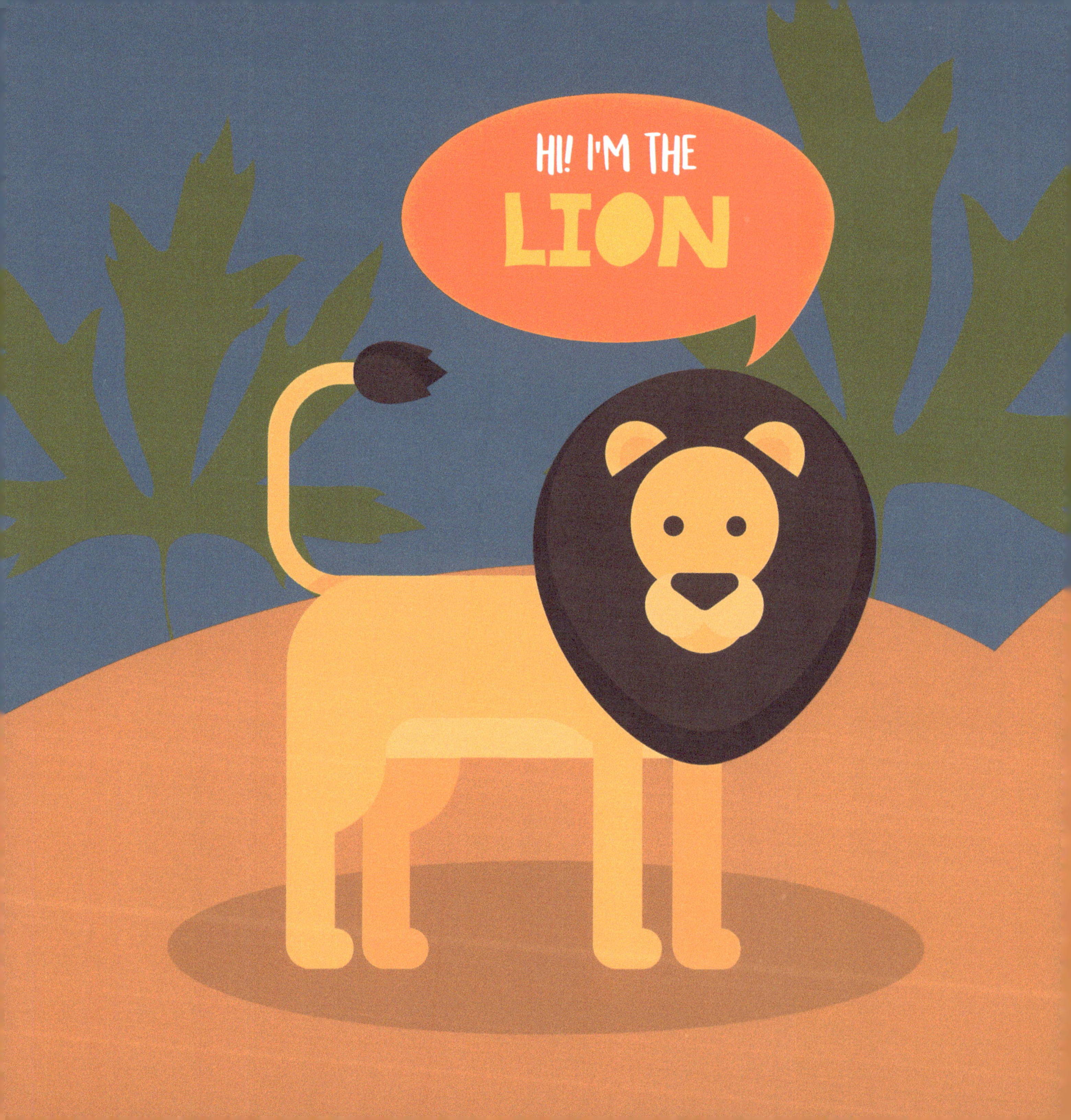
HI! I'M THE
LION

WE USE OUR ROAR TO COMMUNICATE WITH OTHER LIONS, AND IT CAN BE HEARD FROM MORE THAN 4 MILES AWAY!

YOU MIGHT BE SURPRISED, BUT WE'RE REALLY LAZY AND CAN SLEEP UP TO 20 HOURS A DAY.

OUR JAWS ARE ONE OF THE DEADLIEST WEAPONS IN NATURE. THEY'RE SUPER STRONG, AND WE CAN OPEN OUR MOUTHS MORE THAN 12 INCHES WIDE.

MY SENSE OF SIGHT IS ABOUT 6 TIMES MORE SENSITIVE THAN A HUMAN'S. DON'T HIDE—I CAN SEE YOU FROM HERE!

WE LIVE IN GROUPS CALLED PRIDES, AND A PRIDE USUALLY HAS AROUND 40 LIONS.

THERE ARE ONLY ABOUT
39.000
LIONS LEFT IN THE WORLD

WE'RE KNOWN FOR OUR SLOWNESS, AND THAT'S BECAUSE WE HAVE VERY LITTLE MUSCLE MASS AND A SUPER SLOW METABOLISM.

THE SHORT HAIR ON OUR FACES GIVES US A PERMANENT SMILE.

I'M A SOLITARY ANIMAL WHO SPENDS MOST OF MY TIME SLEEPING (AN AVERAGE OF 9.6 HOURS A DAY) AND EATING IN THE TREETOPS. AHH, SUCH RELAXATION!

IF YOU LOOK CLOSELY, YOU'LL SEE GREEN SPOTS ON MY BODY. DO YOU KNOW WHY? IT'S BECAUSE ALGAE GROW IN MY FUR!

I MOVE SO SLOWLY THAT IT'S HARD TO TELL IF I'M SLEEPING OR MOVING. EVERYTHING HAS TO BE TAKEN SLOWLY!

THERE ARE LESS THAN

500

PYGMY SLOTHS LEFT IN THE WORLD

I ABSOLUTELY LOVE BAMBOO AND CAN SPEND MORE THAN HALF THE DAY JUST TASTING AND ENJOYING IT. I NEED TO EAT AT LEAST 26 POUNDS OF BAMBOO EVERY DAY!

WE HAVE SEVEN TIMES MORE TEETH THAN HUMANS.
BIG TEETH THAT MAKE IT EASIER TO CHEW BAMBOO—DID I MENTION I LOVE IT?

WE ARE SOLITARY ANIMALS.
WE LIKE HAVING MOST OF THE FOREST TO OURSELVES BECAUSE WE DON'T HAVE ENOUGH ENERGY TO COMPETE WITH OTHER PANDAS FOR FOOD, TERRITORY, OR MATES. LIVE AND LET LIVE!

WE DON'T HIBERNATE LIKE OTHER BEARS.

THERE ARE ONLY ABOUT

1864

PANDA BEARS LEFT IN THE WORLD

AREN'T THEY ALL AMAZING?
NOW YOU MIGHT BE THINKING, "WHAT CAN I DO TO SAVE THEM? I'M JUST A KID!"
WELL, YOU CAN DO A LOT!

THE FIRST THING IS TO TELL EVERYONE WHAT YOU'VE LEARNED SO YOUR FRIENDS AND FAMILY CAN ALSO KNOW HOW AWESOME THESE ANIMALS ARE—AND HOW THEY ARE IN DANGER!

THAT WAY, TOGETHER, WE CAN CHANGE THE BAD HABITS THAT ARE DESTROYING THE PLANET, AND IN TURN, HELP MANY ANIMAL SPECIES, AS WELL AS OUR OWN WELL-BEING AND FUTURE.

EACH ANIMAL SPECIES FACES ITS OWN SET OF DANGERS, BUT IN GENERAL, THEIR WORST ENEMIES ARE POACHING AND THE DESTRUCTION OF THEIR HABITATS, THE PLACES WHERE THEY LIVE.

SO WHAT CAN YOU DO TO HELP TAKE CARE OF THE PLANET?

FOLLOW THESE TIPS AND SHARE THEM WITH YOUR FRIENDS AND FAMILY:

SAVE ENERGY BY TURNING OFF LIGHTS WHEN THEY'RE NOT NEEDED AND UNPLUGGING THINGS LIKE YOUR GAME CONSOLE, COMPUTER, AND TV...

REDUCE THE AMOUNT OF TRASH YOU CREATE, SUCH AS PAPER, AND USE LESS WATER (TURN OFF THE TAP WHEN YOU'RE NOT USING IT AND TAKE SHOWERS INSTEAD OF BATHS).

BUY LOCAL FOOD WHENEVER POSSIBLE.
YOU'LL SUPPORT LOCAL FARMERS, AND IT WILL REDUCE THE CARBON EMISSIONS FROM TRANSPORTING FOOD FROM THE OTHER SIDE OF THE COUNTRY OR THE WORLD.

Recycle all the materials you can, from paper to clothes and even your toys. There are many things that can be reused or given a new life. Use your imagination and donate what you no longer use.

Use recycling bins.

Reduce, reuse, recycle.

www.ingramcontent.com/pod-product-compliance
Lightning Source LLC
LaVergne TN
LVHW070540070526
838199LV00076B/6814